Copyright © 2022 by Spring Arbor University Press

All rights reserved. No part of this publication may be reproduced, stored in a retrieval system, or transmitted, in any form or by any means (electronic, mechanical, photocopying, recording or otherwise), without the prior written permission of the publisher.

First paperback edition February 2022
Spring Arbor University Press

Spring Arbor University
106 E. Main St.
Spring Arbor, MI 49283

ISBN 979-8-9853982-0-5 (paperback)

Library of Congress Control Number: 2021924278

Edited by Chris Iott
social-sound.com

Printed and bound by Gilson Graphics, Grand Rapids, MI
gilsongraphics.com

Cover design and typeset by Marla Sanford

www.arbor.edu

Grace and Truth

GRACE
AND
TRUTH

Enjoy and download digital versions of this book or request multiple copies by scanning the code below with the camera app on your smartphone.

SCAN HERE

CONTENTS

FOREWORD
5

INTRODUCTION
7

ONE
What is Truth? 13

TWO
Jesus 21

THREE
The Bible 31

FOUR
God and Creation 43

FIVE
Human Relationship and Responsibility 51

SIX
Sin and its Consequences 59

SEVEN
Redemption and Reconciliation 71

EIGHT
This is Grace 81

NINE
Response to Mercy: Personal Transformation 87

TEN
The Holy Spirit and Sanctification 95

ELEVEN
Ambassadors of Christ 105

TWELVE
Gospel = Grace + Truth 111

REFERENCES
129

FOREWORD

I have had the privilege of working closely with Dr. Brent Ellis for many years, watching his tireless efforts to help shape the operations and vision for the next generation of success at Spring Arbor University (SAU). In the spring of 2021, I was able to participate in all five of SAU's Commencement celebrations, and at one of those ceremonies, Dr. Ellis delivered the Commencement address and spoke about the need to effectively merge grace and truth to properly pursue the Gospel's direction for all of us. I was moved. Dr. Ellis presented a clear and vital message particularly salient for our time, and I encouraged him to further focus and expound upon that topic going forward.

While most institutions of higher education – including Christian colleges and universities like Spring Arbor University – currently face many challenges, and our society in general is becoming increasingly polarized and fragmented into entrenched competing factions, Dr. Ellis brings a clear call to healing and reconciliation through a thoughtful application of the true Gospel message. We must find better ways to merge both **grace** and **truth** in all our communications, relationships, and interactions with others to effectively live out and share the Gospel of Jesus Christ.

Dale E. Stephenson
Chairman, Board of Trustees
Spring Arbor University
Summer 2021

INTRODUCTION

Even though I was raised in a devout Christian home, my conversion occurred during my freshman year in college. Within the first several weeks there, the collision of the claims of Christ against my self-created view of God came into full conflict and resulted in the surrender of my will to the will of our Heavenly Father. From that time forward, my life focus has centered on the growth of my own faith as well as teaching/sharing the "reason for the hope" I possess (1 Peter 3:15). For the past 30-plus years, my educational and career decisions focused on this commitment. This journey led me into Christian higher education, where I have had the privilege of working alongside gifted men and women who impact, influence, and educate tens of thousands of students, then send them into the world to serve as outstanding professionals who use their education, networks, family relationships and the like to impact our world for Christ and His Kingdom. The stories of these alumni and their service to God in our world inspire me and give me great hope for the future of our world.

Yet today, even with the significant work of Christian colleges and universities along with the global Church, we find ourselves within an increasingly secular culture. In a recent poll, 43% of millennials said they either don't know, don't care, or don't believe God exists. In the same poll, only 16% said they believe they will go to heaven because they have confessed their sins and accepted Jesus as their Savior. These statistics, while sobering, provide a glimpse into a world ready to hear the message of the Gospel. My desire in writing this study guide is to provide a resource to those desiring to make the Gospel known to our world.

John, the disciple of Jesus, wrote in 1 John 1:14, "The Word became flesh and made His dwelling among us. We have seen His glory, the glory of the One and Only, who came from the Father, full of grace and truth." Our efforts in making the Gospel of Jesus Christ known to the world, require us to mirror the manner in which Jesus Himself encountered His

INTRODUCTION

creation, full of grace and truth. If I could offer one broad critique of the modern Church, it would be that often we offer either grace or truth, not grace *and* truth. I am certain you have observed the harsh judgment of Christians decrying the sinful offenses of the world in hostile and angry postures. Along with this picture, you have also observed Christians abandoning the teachings of the Holy Bible in hopes their words do not offend their audience. The result can lead to confusion and frustration.

As Christians, if we merely offer the grace of God, with no understanding or grounding in truth of God, we mirror the broader culture of relativism where every action and every deed is justified by individual preference and internal authenticity. Internal authenticity becomes the greatest good, where a person strives to be true to his or her own particular motives, desires, and passions. If a person can align his/her behavior and life priorities with one's own individual motives, desires, and passions, that person is living with internal authenticity. Grace not coupled with Truth allows people to live within their sinfulness and depravity with no understanding of their need for a Savior.

On the other hand, if Christians merely offer truth, then we mirror the Pharisees of the New Testament or the legalistic perversions of authentic Christian faith and heap burdens upon ourselves and others that no individual can bear. The result leads to individuals believing that salvation is based on self-discipline and one's ability to live in full accordance with the laws of God. Self-righteousness or despair results and leads to judgmental attitudes toward others and our world.

Both of these points of emphasis, *grace without truth* and *truth without grace*, represent perversions of the Gospel and will never result in impacting our world in the manner God desires. The Gospel message is powerful because it is not one or the other, but both grace and truth. My hope, through this writing, is to provide a high-level reminder of the complete Gospel message of Christ. Jesus came full of grace and truth; if we are to serve as His ambassadors to the world, we too, must come to the world full of grace and truth.

INTRODUCTION

To best understand grace, we first need to understand truth.

GRACE AND TRUTH

CHAPTER ONE

WHAT IS TRUTH?

What is truth? This is not a new question, but one which inquisitive people from the beginning of creation have contemplated. Pontius Pilate, in response to Jesus's statement that he had come to earth to testify to the Truth, retorted, "What is Truth?" (John 18:38). Even the exchange between the serpent and Eve recorded in Genesis 3 reflects a twisting of truth. Genesis 2:16-17 expresses God's desire for Adam as he acted as caretaker of the Garden of Eden. God said, "You are free to eat from any tree in the garden; but you must not eat from the tree of the knowledge of good and evil, for when you eat of it you will surely die." Genesis 3 then records both the serpent's twisting of truth as well as Eve's lack of understanding truth. The serpent questions, "Did God really say, 'You must not eat from any tree in the garden'?" (Genesis 3:1). Eve responds, "We may eat fruit from the trees in the garden, but God did say, 'You must not eat fruit from the tree that is in the middle of the garden, and you must not touch it, or you will die.'" (Genesis 3:2-3). The serpent twists truth into a lie and Eve adds to the command by stating God said not to even touch the fruit or you will die. In both cases, truth was not articulated.

So how do we know truth? Volumes of writings unpack this question; theories abound that attempt to provide frameworks for discovering truth. The *Correspondence Theory* is perhaps the most well known. It basically states that truth corresponds to the facts. If something corresponds to observable facts, then it is truth. Many other modern and postmodern theorists have expanded or even argued against this theory. In one of my very first doctoral classes at Indiana University, my professor began the class with this statement, "Christians are the most ignorant people on the face of the earth. They believe they know absolute truth, but they cannot; therefore, they are the most ignorant people on the face of the earth." The class was a qualitative research class. The professor went on to explain scientific truth (H_2O is always water), mathematical truth (2+2=4), empirical truth (what can be observed or measured) and metaphysical truth (transcendent personal perceptions).

As I sat in the lecture, I remember praying for an opportunity to engage this professor in some manner. When the time was right, I raised my hand and expressed to the professor and my classmates that I was a Christian and would like to explore his first statement regarding Christians being "the most ignorant people on the face of the earth" a little further. I asked him whether he planned to duck as we exited the building after class. He responded by asking, "Why would I duck?" I stated that it was possible that he could be hit in the head by a frisbee; while not probable, it was definitely possible. He laughed and I then went on to explain that he was correct in asserting that Christians cannot prove through mathematical, scientific, or empirical truth that Jesus is the son of God. But we can explore possibilities and probabilities leading to a confident conclusion.

Jesus said, "I am the way, the truth, and the life. No one comes to the Father but by me" (John

14:6). This statement is either true or it is false. Jesus is either the only way to God the Father or He is not. While we cannot use certain forms of inquiry to test the validity of this claim, we can look at possibilities and probabilities. I related to my professor and classmates that as I examined all the information regarding Jesus, while there is a possibility He is not who He claimed to be, all probability pointed to the fact that He is indeed the Son of the Living God. Therefore, I align the entirety of my life with the belief that Jesus is who He claimed to be, and that truth becomes absolute for me. The professor thanked me for this explanation and said he had never had a Christian unpack this with him before. Three years later that professor served as the methodologist for my doctoral dissertation.

The legal system of the United States of America utilizes this same standard for juries in criminal cases. The prosecution must prove a defendant's guilt beyond all reasonable doubt. This standard does not mean there can be no doubt, but the jury must be convinced of the defendant's guilt

WHAT IS TRUTH?

beyond all reasonable doubt. While we may not be able to prove through scientific inquiry the validity of Jesus's claims, we are able, through exploration of what we do understand about Jesus, His life and death and resurrection, that He is indeed the Son of God.

Chapter One
Reflection Questions

Key Point
Truth exists and can be determined through the examination of possibilities and probabilities.

---

1) Why does the idea of truth matter?

2) What do you believe to be true that cannot be proven scientifically or mathematically?

3) How do you decide something is true enough to influence your behavior?

Personal Perspective
Write your own reaction to the thoughts communicated within this chapter.

NOTES

GRACE AND TRUTH

CHAPTER TWO

JESUS

Perhaps there is need to take a step back and walk through several of the factual aspects of the life of Jesus of Nazareth that led me to base the totality of my life on the belief that Jesus is exactly who He claimed to be. Historically, Jesus is a well-documented person. The Bible itself provides significant documentation about Jesus of Nazareth and His birth, death, and resurrection. The four gospels provide this detail, and several of the letters written by Paul, Peter, John, James, and Jude also provide details about the life of Jesus. Luke's gospel is perhaps the most "historical" in nature.

In Luke 1:3, he writes, "Therefore, since I myself have carefully investigated everything from the beginning, it seemed good also for me to write an orderly account for you, most excellent Theophilus, so that you may know the certainty of the things you have been taught." John concludes his gospel with this statement, "Jesus did many other things as well. If every one of them were written down, I suppose that even the whole world would not have room for the books that would be written." The Bible itself provides great detail about the life of Jesus. However, exclusively utilizing the Bible to prove the claims of the Bible is limited. Fortunately, there are several historical records of Jesus of Nazareth that exist beyond the biblical text.

Flavius Josephus, a Jewish historian who wrote a history of the Jews for the Roman Empire called *Antiquities of the Jews*, mentions Jesus in two separate books of his history. In Book 18 Jesus is recorded as being crucified by Pontius Pilate, and in Book 20 Josephus mentions "the brother of Jesus, who was called the Christ, whose name was James." While Flavius Josephus was not a disciple of Jesus, he was certain that Jesus of Nazareth did exist, was crucified at the hands of Pontius Pilate, and that Jesus's brother was James, one of the heads of the early Christian movement. Again, this documentation of the historical Jesus does not prove Jesus's claims but provides further evidence of His existence as well as validating the biblical text.

JESUS

A second, non-biblical source is from Tacitus, a Roman Senator and historian. In his history of the Roman Empire titled *Annals*, he references Christ as he describes what led to the Great Fire of Rome in 64 AD Tacitus writes,

> *"Nero fastened the guilt and inflicted the most exquisite tortures on a class hated for their abominations, called Christians by the populace. Christus, from whom the name had its origin, suffered the extreme penalty during the reign of Tiberius at the hands of one of our procurators, Pontius Pilatus, and a most mischievous superstition, thus checked for the moment, again broke out not only in Judea, the first source of the evil, but even in Rome"* (Annals, 15.44).

Again, while Tacitus did not believe that Jesus was the Son of the living God, he did believe that Jesus of Nazareth lived, was crucified by Pontius Pilate, and that a movement that believed Jesus rose from the dead and was the Son of the Living God began in Judea and spread even to Rome.

A third mention, not intended to be a historical account, is a letter written by Pliny the

Younger, who was a Roman Governor. He wrote to Emperor Trajan seeking counsel on how to handle individuals who believed "Christ was a god," and he provides a thorough description of the early church and how they worshipped. Again, Pliny the Younger did not believe Jesus of Nazareth was God, but he did believe that Jesus of Nazareth existed and that many people living in his province worshipped Jesus as God.

Historically, there is no doubt that Jesus of Nazareth existed as a real person. The question then is not whether Jesus lived, but whether Jesus was who He claimed to be. Here are four facts we know are true about the life of Jesus:

1) Jesus of Nazareth existed. He was a real person.

2) Jesus of Nazareth was executed by the Roman Empire under the direction of Pontius Pilate.

3) Jesus of Nazareth did indeed die as a result of His crucifixion.

4) Jesus's disciples and those who knew Him best, including His half-brothers James and Jude, truly believed that He rose from the dead and were completely convinced He was exactly who He claimed to be, the Son of the Living God.

The fourth historical point provided above is important to develop further in exploring the question around the veracity of Jesus's claims. We do know with certainty that Jesus's disciples, those who knew Him best along with James and Jude believed Jesus rose from the dead and was indeed the Messiah, the Son of the Living God. The apostle Paul describes this in 1 Corinthians 15:3-8, writing,

"For what I received I passed on to you as of first importance: that Christ died for our sins according to the Scriptures, that He was buried, that He was raised on the third day according to the Scriptures, and that He appeared to Peter, then to the Twelve. After that, He appeared to more than five hundred of the brothers at the same time, most of whom are still living, though some have fallen asleep. Then He appeared to

James, then to all the apostles, and last of all He appeared to me also, as one abnormally born."

These men and women who saw the resurrected Jesus were convinced to the point that they went out and changed the world. All of Jesus's disciples, including James and Paul, were either imprisoned or executed because they believed Jesus was who He claimed to be. None of these individuals experienced financial gain or saw their social standing increase. Instead, persecution, suffering and death awaited these individuals. Yet they were willing to walk through these hardships and endure these punishments because they were convinced that Jesus was the Messiah, the Son of the Living God. Sane people do not choose to suffer and die for a lie they themselves created. Thousands of early Christians chose to die because they were convinced Jesus was God.

Perhaps the argument that is most compelling to me, utilized frequently by C.S. Lewis, is called the *Trilemma*. This argument addresses those who believe Jesus of Nazareth was indeed a real person and a great teacher or even prophet of God, but not the Messiah. Basically, the argument boils down to three options for considering who Jesus was. The Bible clearly records Jesus asserting that He was indeed the Messiah and is God. A person who claims to be God cannot be a good teacher or prophet of God. He is one of three things: a lunatic, a liar, or Lord. C.S. Lewis writes in his book, *Mere Christianity*, "Now it seems to me obvious that He was neither a lunatic nor a fiend: and consequently, however strange or terrifying or unlikely it may seem, I have to accept the view that He was and is God" (pp. 55-56). The argument is fairly simple: Jesus claimed to be God. He is either who He claimed to be, or He is a liar or a lunatic. The life of Jesus, recorded in the Bible, does not in any way indicate that Jesus was a liar or a lunatic. Therefore, Jesus was and is who He claimed to be—God.

Chapter Two
Reflection Questions

Key Point
Jesus's existence is well documented, with strong evidence of His claims.

---

1) Unique events are, by definition, unlikely. How do you evaluate unlikely claims that people make?
2) If highly unlikely claims are "impossible," what would cause you to believe them?
3) Which of the five arguments for the historicity of Jesus outlined in this chapter is most compelling to you? Why?

Personal Perspective
Write your own reaction to the thoughts communicated within this chapter.

NOTES

GRACE AND TRUTH

CHAPTER THREE

THE BIBLE

Another question to ponder, prior to delving deeper into what the Bible teaches as truth, is Why can we trust the Bible? Yet another question: What is the Bible? Many postmodern scholars believe the Bible is merely a collection of writings meant to control and manipulate populations to act and behave in a manner that allows those in control to stay in control. If this were true, I would not want to follow its teachings either. Faithful Christians, on the other hand, believe the Bible to be the inspired Word of God, perfect in what it teaches, and authoritative for the lives of disciples of Christ. Again, these two positions cannot be established through scientific or mathematical endeavors.

A few points of observation help provide the rationale behind why we can be certain that the Bible is indeed the very Word of God. One element is the fulfillment of prophecy throughout the Old Testament. From the nation of Israel being established through the offspring of Abraham and the conquest of the Promised Land, to the exile of Israel and Judah to Assyria and Babylon, time and time again, the prophecies of the Old Testament are fulfilled and recorded historically. The most significant fulfillment of multiple prophesies are the prophesies associated with the Messiah and their fulfillment in the life of Jesus of Nazareth. The Old Testament is full of fulfilled prophecies concerning the Messiah. Consider these few examples:

Micah 5:2 – *"But you, Bethlehem Ephrathah, though you are small among the clans of Judah, out of you will come for me one who will be ruler over Israel, whose origins are from of old, from ancient times."*

Isaiah 7:14 – *"Therefore the Lord himself will give you a sign: The virgin will conceive and give birth to a son, and will call him Immanuel."*

Isaiah 53:3-5 – *"He was despised and rejected by men, A man of great suffering and familiar with pain. Like one from whom people hide their faces, He was despised, and we held him in low esteem. However, it was our sickness that He Himself bore, and our pains that He carried. Yet* *we ourselves assumed that He had been afflicted, struck down by God and humiliated. But he was pierced for our transgressions, He was crushed for our wrongdoings. The punishment for our well-being was laid upon Him and by His wounds we are healed."*

The vast number of fulfilled prophesies contained within the Bible, approximately 2,000 in number, are significant evidence of the reliability of the Bible as the inspired and authoritative Word of God.

Another reason we can trust the veracity of the Bible is the internal consistency of both the Old and New Testaments. The field of Textual Criticism exists because we do not have the original writing (the autograph) of any book of the Bible. What we do possess are multiple manuscripts and fragments of manuscripts that have been handed down and preserved through thousands of years. Most people are aware of the Dead Sea Scrolls found in the mid-20th century in several caves close to the Dead Sea. Like these manuscripts and fragments of manuscripts found, there are thousands of such documents that exist and are preserved around the world. Within these thousands of manuscripts, there are remarkably few internal inconsistencies. In fact, when the Dead Sea Scrolls were discovered, many believed there would be significant evidence of tampering and changing the text of the Old Testament Scripture. Instead, only a few and very minor variants were found.

During a trip to Israel, the tour guide leading our group explained his perspective on why there were very limited and minor variants found after the discovery of the Dead Sea Scrolls. His theory was that Jewish people from Jerusalem must have placed them in this location during the fall of Jerusalem in 70 AD, because if the people of Essen had written them, they would have invariably written themselves into their Scriptures as heroes of the faith. I retorted that perhaps a second theory is also possible. The Essenes were a group of Israelites committed to the preservation of the Jewish Scriptures and intentionally chose to live communal lives in isolation from the general population. Perhaps the consistency of the texts produced by the Essenes is so remarkably thorough because of the high regard these people had for the Word of God and that changing, even slightly, the Word of God would be an abdication and rejection of their faith. Jesus taught as much stating, "For truly I tell you, until heaven and earth disappear, not the smallest letter, not the least stroke of a pen, will by any means disappear from the Law until everything is accomplished" (Matthew 5:18).

The Jewish people have preserved the Holy Scriptures so well, the internal consistency of the Bible is nearly impeccable. This is true across all the manuscripts that exist. The variants that do exist are typically very minor and most often add some type of detail to help explain something in the text. Within the academic discipline of Textual Criticism, the foundational step is to always assume the simplest and shortest of two variants is closest to the original. The internal consistency of the Holy Scripture is another piece of evidence in helping us understand that the Bible is indeed the inspired and authoritative Word of God.

Finally, archaeological findings have exclusively verified the history of what is written in the Bible. Visiting the Holy Land a few years back, the consistency of the Bible's history with what has and is currently being discovered by archaeologists throughout the Middle East is staggering. Each discovery validates with greater clarity the reliability of the Scriptures. Through these observable facts, fulfillment of prophecy, internal consistency, and archaeological findings—in addition to what the Bible says about itself—we can be confident that what the Bible teaches is true, reliable, and authoritative for the life of believers. The apostle Paul, in 2 Timothy 3:16-17, states, "All Scripture is God-breathed and beneficial for teaching, rebuking, correcting, and training in righteousness, so that the servant of God might be thoroughly equipped for every good work."

In order to capture this broader commitment, many groups have attempted to articulate a statement of belief regarding the Bible. The *Lausanne Covenant*, signed by hundreds of church leaders in the 20th century, attempted to capture shared perspectives of the Christian faith. The statement made by this group regarding the authority and power of the Bible states,

"We affirm the divine inspiration, truthfulness and authority of both Old and New Testament Scriptures in their entirety as the only written word of God, without error in all that it affirms, and the only infallible rule of faith and practice. We also affirm the power of God's word to accomplish his purpose of salvation. The message of the Bible is addressed to all men and women. For God's revelation in Christ and in Scripture is unchangeable. Through it the Holy Spirit still speaks today. He illumines the minds of God's people in every culture to perceive its truth freshly through their own eyes and thus discloses to the whole Church ever more of the many-cool red wisdom of God."

The Free Methodist Church (my personal denomination) communicates a similar perspective in its *Book of Discipline*,

"The Bible is God's written Word, uniquely inspired by the Holy Spirit. It bears unerring witness to Jesus Christ, the living Word. As attested by the early church and subsequent councils, it is the trustworthy record of God's revelation, completely truthful in all it affirms. It has been faithfully preserved and proves itself true in human experience.

The Scriptures have come to us through human authors who wrote, as God moved them, in the languages and literary forms of their times. God continues, by the illumination of the Holy Spirit, to speak through this Word to each generation and culture.

The Bible has authority over all human life. It teaches the truth about God, His creation, His people, His one and only Son and the destiny of humankind. It also teaches the way of salvation and the life of faith. Whatever is not found in the Bible nor can be proved by it is not to be required as an article of belief or as necessary to salvation" (Paragraph 108).

Anselm, a Catholic philosopher and

theologian, wrote about the Bible, "For I am sure that, if I say anything which is undoubtedly contradictory to Holy Scripture, it is wrong" (*Anselm of Canterbury*, 298). We, too, affirm that the Bible provides perspective and understanding for believers regarding God, His creation, humanity, sin, redemption, reconciliation, and all that is necessary for a Christian to walk faithfully with God. As Anselm beautifully articulates, when society and culture hold positions or opinions contrary to the teaching and witness of the Holy Scriptures, the Holy Scriptures carry truth and therefore authority for the lives of believers.

Chapter Three
Reflection Questions

Key Point
The Bible is the very Word of God, evidenced by fulfillment of prophecy, internal consistency, and archaeology.

---

1) What does the Bible claim for itself? With what evidence?

2) If not an objective source such as the Bible, on what basis do you make decisions about spiritual matters?

3) How do you respond to others who, unlike Anselm, believe there might be inconsistencies within Scripture?

4) How has your engagement with the Scriptures impacted your daily life? Your relationships?

Personal Perspective
Write your own reaction to the thoughts communicated within this chapter.

NOTES

GRACE AND TRUTH

CHAPTER FOUR

GOD AND CREATION

With a foundational and fundamental understanding that Jesus is indeed who He claimed to be and that the Bible is the inspired and authoritative Word of God, we can begin exploring what the Bible teaches about God, humanity, sin, redemption, and the life of a disciple of Christ.

The Bible begins with perhaps the most essential aspect of our understanding of existence, "In the beginning God created the heavens and the earth" (Genesis 1:1). Clearly from this single statement we can deduce that God existed before creation and exists outside of creation. While our knowledge and understanding are limited by what we observe within the created realm, God's knowledge and understanding contain no limits based upon time, space, and what can be observed. Within the creation narrative, it is also clear that God created all that exists with intelligence and intentionality. While there are great debates within the Christian church as to the purpose of Genesis 1 and 2, there is universal agreement around these particular truths:

1) God is eternal and existed prior to the creation of the universe.

2) God created all that exists with intentionality and purpose.

3) Humans serve in a special and unique position relative to all other aspects of creation, to serve as stewards of God's creation.

Consider for the moment the consistent description of the various aspects of the creation "according to its kind" or "according to their kind." This description is provided referring to trees, plants, sea creatures, birds, livestock, wild animals, and animals that move along the ground (Genesis 1:11, 12, 21, 24, 25). The intentionality of this type of creation is important to note. God intentionally created these types of vegetation and these types of animals. He made them "according to its kind" or "according to their kind." An aspect to consider here is the reality that as we explore and work to gain greater understanding of our world, how it functions and sustains life as well as understanding aspects of creation through the sciences and the social sciences, we gain greater understanding of the mind of God.

As a university president, I regularly remind our students and faculty of the fact that regardless of one's field of study, as we seek understanding and knowledge about our world, we are uncovering and understanding with greater clarity the very mind of God. I particularly love the refrained statement of a retired biology professor as he oversaw Spring Arbor University students participating in their laboratory exercises. As he walked between these students dissecting frogs or observing cell structures of plants, he would proclaim, "Students, this is worship!"

The opportunity we have to observe and gain understanding and clarity around aspects of God's creation is a wonderful gift to humanity. As Christians, we should never fear inquiry or study but should eagerly seek greater understanding and discovery because the more we understand God's creation the more we understand our God.

As the pinnacle of God's intelligent and intentional creative act, He chose to make human beings. Genesis 1:26-27 states,

"Then God said, 'Let us make man in our image, in our likeness, and let them rule over the fish of the sea and the birds of the air, over the livestock, over all the earth, and over all the creatures that move along the ground.' So, God created man in his own image, in the image of God He created him; male and female, He created them."

Within these two verses, two items should be noted. The first is the fact that human beings, out of all created things, are exclusively made in the image and the likeness of God. No other created thing mentioned in Genesis Chapter 1 carries this same description. Vegetation, animals, the heavens, and the earth are all created "according to its kind." Humanity, however, is created, not "according to its kind" but rather in the image and the likeness of God. The second is the fact that humanity carries a charge from our Creator to care for His creation as a steward. We will unpack this second aspect when we examine

GOD AND CREATION

Human Responsibility, but before we understand our responsibility, we must first understand our creation as image bearers of the Creator.

The *imago Dei* (God's image bearer) is a profound concept that requires full consideration: Out of all that was made, the only created thing bearing the image and likeness of God Himself is humanity. Implicit within this truth is the fact that every human to ever exist, born or unborn, is an image bearer of the Creator God. Any attempt to elevate one race, ethnicity, or nationality over another is an affront to the understanding that all people are image bearers of God. As image bearers, every person to ever exist is implicitly valuable and worthy of dignity and respect.

Chapter Four
Reflection Questions

Key Point

God exists before and outside of creation, and He created all things according to their kind – except human beings, which were created in God's own image.

---

1) The Bible says the first something was God. Does it matter to that claim exactly how God chose to create everything else?

2) What do you think it means to be created in the image of God? How are human beings different from all other creatures? How are all human beings alike, despite observable differences?

3) In what ways is the exploration of our world and our relationships an act or posture of worship?

Personal Perspective

Write your own reaction to the thoughts communicated within this chapter.

NOTES

GRACE AND TRUTH

CHAPTER FIVE

HUMAN RELATIONSHIP AND RESPONSIBILITY

With the understanding that humans are exclusively the image bearers of God, the second component can be explored. Humanity bears responsibility for creation, as indicated in the statement, "Let them rule over the fish of the sea and the birds of the air." The Hebrew word translated to "rule" in this verse means to have dominion over. Like the exclusive aspect of humanity being created in the image and likeness of God, so too, no other aspect of creation is charged with the responsibility of dominion or rule over creation. What does this mean for humanity? It means that just as God created all things with intelligence and intentionality, we as His image bearers must act within our world with intelligence and intentionality, caring for God's creation in a manner that reflects the intent in God's creative act. This is God's creation and God's world, not humanity's world. As His image bearers, we are asked to rule over God's world in a manner consistent with God's character and intent in creation.

The implications of this commission are enormous. While there may be wide disagreement as to the proper manner to approach stewardship of the earth, there is no room for a committed Christian to abdicate his/her responsibility to act as a caregiver and steward of God's creation. The Bible is filled with references and metaphors concerning the care of our world. One verse to consider is Exodus 23:10-11. Moses has led the Israelites out of bondage in Egypt and God has provided Moses the Ten Commandments. This verse comes within the context of Moses communicating God's will and intent for the people of Israel as they take possession of the promised land. The verse reads,

"For six years you are to sow your fields and harvest your crops, but during the seventh year let the land lie unplowed and unused. Then the poor among your people may get food from it, and the wild animals may eat what they leave. Do the same with your vineyard and your olive grove."

These two verses provide excellent insight

into the application of God's commission for humanity to act as stewards and caregivers of His creation. The stated intent of the year of rest for the land communicates God's desire for humanity to care for each other. The idea of care for the poor and vulnerable is a hallmark of the Bible, and James states, "pure and faultless" religion "looks after widows and orphans in distress" (James 1:27). The sociological aspect of humanity's "rule" over God's creation is clearly communicated within these verses from Exodus. A secondary motive communicated as well is care and provision for animals. The New International Version translates the Hebrew word for "beasts" into wild animals. What we can also clearly understand from this verse is the fact that God also desires us to be mindful of the care and provision for animals. Finally, these aspects of care are provided through the practice of fallowing land every seven years. From a scientific perspective, the practice of fallowing land has been shown to increase the ability of soil to produce and grow crops.

    Creation stewardship and care are a significant

charge. In Genesis 2, the weight of this responsibility is recognized and reinforced by God. In order to carry out the responsibilities associated with this significant charge, God intentionally created males and females. Genesis 2:20-24 states,

> *"But for Adam no suitable helper was found. So, the Lord God caused the man to fall into a deep sleep and while he was sleeping, He took one of the man's ribs and closed up the place with flesh. Then the Lord God made woman from the rib He had taken out of the man and brought her to the man. The man said, 'This is now bone of my bone and flesh of my flesh; she shall be called woman for she was taken out of man.' For this reason, a man will leave his father and mother and be united to his wife, and they will become one flesh."*

The importance of these verses cannot be overstated. It is from these verses that Jews and Christians derive their perspectives on marriage.

Dr. Timothy Tennent, in his book, *For the Body*, writes regarding this passage, "For Christians, marriage is a covenantal union of two genders brought into a one-flesh relationship: two different glories coming together to make one new glorious unity" (pg. 50). Jesus Himself makes mention of this passage when asked by the Pharisees whether it is lawful for a man to divorce his wife. Jesus's response to the question reads,

> *"Haven't you read that at the beginning the Creator 'made them male and female,' and said, 'For this reason a man will leave his father and mother and be united to his wife, and the two will become one flesh'? So they are no longer two, but one flesh. Therefore, what God has joined together, let no one separate"* (Matthew 19:4-6).

A Christian perspective on marriage is derived from these verses, understanding the importance of both genders becoming one in purpose and function. Suitable partners coming together to carry out the responsibility of ruling over or having dominion over creation, as well as being fruitful and multiplying (Genesis 1:28), is central to the Christian purpose of marriage. One man and one woman joined together through a covenant before God for the purpose of carrying out the intent of God in caring for and leading His creation is the Christian view of marriage.

Chapter Five
Reflection Questions

Key Point
Humanity bears responsibility for creation and to care for it as God intended.

---

1) What authority and responsibility did God give to Adam? How did God support Adam in this responsibility?

2) What are the implications of God creating male and female as well as establishing marriage and families?

3) To what extent does your own creativity, leadership, and relationship-building reflect the "intelligence and intentionality" of God's creative activity?

Personal Perspective
Write your own reaction to the thoughts communicated within this chapter.

GRACE AND TRUTH

CHAPTER SIX

SIN AND ITS CONSEQUENCES

Our world did not remain perfect, as we discussed earlier. The serpent twisted truth and Eve added to truth, leading to a disobedient act where both Adam and Eve ate the fruit of the Tree of the Knowledge of Good and Evil. Through this disobedient act, God's perfect creation became corrupt and fallen. Paul explains the ramifications of this act in Romans 5:12, "Therefore, just as sin entered the world through one man, and death through sin, and in this way death came to all people, because all have sinned."

Romans 1 outlines the consequences of the fall of humanity with even greater clarity. Paul begins with a broad statement about the wrath of God being revealed against the wickedness of humanity who suppress truth by sinful actions (Romans 1:18). He outlines three broad categorical consequences of the fall of humanity: (1) sinful desires of the heart, (2) lusts of the flesh, and (3) a depraved mind. Romans

1:21-24 contains a description of the first category, sinful desires of their hearts,

> *"For although they knew God, they neither glorified him as God nor gave thanks to him, but their thinking became futile, and their foolish hearts were darkened. Although they claimed to be wise, they became fools and exchanged the glory of the immortal God for images made to look like mortal man and birds and animals and reptiles.* ***Therefore, God gave them over in the sinful desires of their hearts*** *to sexual impurity for the degrading of their bodies with one another."*
> (Emphasis added.)

The first consequence for not worshipping God as God is being given over to the sinful desires of our hearts. The example of this consequence is sexual impurity. This example is broad and includes any sort of sexual activity beyond what God intended in establishing marriage between one man and one woman. The category of sinful desires of our hearts is even more broad. We all have sinful desires of our hearts that are manifested in behaviors extending well beyond sexual acts. The point is our hearts are damaged and darkened. Jeremiah 17:9 states, "The heart is more deceitful above all things and beyond cure. Who can understand it?" The desires or inclinations that are most basic to a person, because of the consequences of the fall, are tainted by sin and inconsistent with the character and the will of God.

The second consequence for not worshipping God as God is being given over to shameful lusts, recorded in Romans 1:25-27. Paul writes,

*"They exchanged the truth about God for a lie and worshipped and served created things rather than the Creator, who is forever praised. Amen. **Because of this, God gave them over to shameful lusts.** Even their women exchanged natural relations for unnatural ones. In the same way men also abandoned natural relations with women and were inflamed with lust for one another. Men committed shameful acts with other men and received in themselves the due penalty for their perversion."* (Emphasis added.)

The example Paul provides for shameful lusts is homosexual behavior. Like the first consequence, "shameful lusts" are not exhaustively defined by this example. It is merely one example, but the category of shameful lusts is much broader and impacts all of humanity, regardless of one's sexual preferences. It is also important to note the example of homosexual behavior utilized in this passage. Non-consensual sexual activity is not mentioned in this passage. The context clearly is women engaging in sexual acts with other women and men engaging in sexual acts with other men. Both instances imply the issue is abandoning God's purpose in creating humans as sexual beings and instead practicing an unnatural form of sexual activity that is inconsistent with God's will and intent for His creation.

While all people might not identify with the example provided by Paul, all people are, however, impacted by shameful lusts where we are attracted or pursue passions that are inconsistent and incompatible with God's intent in creation. The prophet Isaiah states, "We all, like sheep, have gone astray, each of us has turned to our own way" (Isaiah 53:6). Our own way is not God's way but is instead described by Paul as shameful lusts. When we pursue our own deep desires, instead of God's will, we enact our shameful lusts.

The final consequence for not worshipping God as God is the depraved mind, described in Romans 1:28-32,

> *"Furthermore, just as they did not think it worthwhile to retain the knowledge of God,* **so God gave them over to a depraved mind***, so that they do what ought not be done. They have become filled with every kind of wickedness, evil, greed, and depravity. They are full of envy, murder, strife, deceit, and malice. They are gossips, slanderers, God-haters, insolent, arrogant and boastful; they invent ways of doing evil; they disobey their parents; they have no understanding, no fidelity, no love, no mercy. Although they know God's righteous decree that those who do such things deserve death, they not only continue to do these very things, but they also approve of those who practice them."* (Emphasis added.)

This third category, depraved mind, contains many examples, but yet again it is not an exhaustive list. The idea conveyed is the fact that even our cognitive ability is impacted by the consequences of sin. People even invent ways of doing evil and approve of those who practice evil. G.K. Chesterton, in an article written for the London News, writes, "Men do not differ much about what things they will call evils; they differ enormously about what evils they will call excusable." Our minds and our thinking, because of the fall of creation, are impacted. All aspects of who we were intended to be through God's gracious creative acts are now corrupted through sin. Compare this with the modern perspective of an "authentic life" or a life where a person lives fully the desires of their heart.

The idea of living an authentically real and transparent life, meaning a person should enact the most basic and carnal aspects of his or her heart's desire, is exactly what this passage describes. As Paul describes the results of humanity not serving God as God, he articulates the fact that God therefore allows humans to instead pursue their own sinful desires and shameful lusts, and then to justify and affirm those actions through the depravity of their minds. Sin, therefore, is the pursuit of an individual's will over the will of God.

Carl Trueman, in his book *The Rise and Triumph of the Modern Self*, explores the dynamics of philosophy, literature, politics, and science that have produced this fallen perspective of humanity over the past several centuries. The term he uses, for which he credits Robert Bellah, is "expressive individualism." Basically, expressive individualism is the idea that a person's most base and carnal instincts are the true nature of a person (Jean-Jacques Rousseau) and that personal happiness is the result of erotic experience (Sigmund Freud). There is nothing beyond what exists in the natural world (Charles Darwin), and any set of external standards that question this reality is a form of oppression and must be overthrown (Karl Marx). The purpose of each individual person, then, is to express his or her authentic individuality. Anything less than expressing individualism is inauthentic and a lie. This "expressive individualism" is an excellent description of what these verses from

Romans 1 articulate.

At times we fall under the delusion that what we face within a modern context is new. But as Ecclesiastes 1:9 reminds us, "There is nothing new under the sun." Our current culture and society reflect what has been common in other times and in other cultures. As Paul makes clear in this passage, God has given humanity over to these base, carnal desires as consequences for not serving Him as God. As we will explore later, God does not desire us to stay within this state; instead, God desires His people to live differently than what is typical of the world.

These consequences of sin are exhaustive throughout humanity. Paul continues his description in Romans 2:1-4, desiring to make certain that all people recognize their sinfulness and need for salvation. He writes,

> *"You, therefore, have no excuse, you who pass judgment on someone else, for at whatever point you judge another, you are condemning yourself, because you who pass judgment do the same things. Now we know that God's judgment against those*

who do such things is based on truth. So, when you, a mere man, pass judgment on them and yet do the same things, do you think you will escape God's judgment? Or do you show contempt for the riches of his kindness, forbearance, and patience, not realizing that God's kindness leads you to repentance?"

The idea of judgment here is not understanding sin as sinful; rather it is believing that others are sinful while you are righteous. The reality is, again to quote Paul from Romans 3:23, that "all have sinned and fall short of the glory of God." Despite the significance of this corruption, there is good news. As Genesis 9 points out, even after the fall and after the flood, Noah is told by God, "Be fruitful and increase in number and fill the earth" (Genesis 9:1), the same call and commission given to Adam and Eve (Genesis 1:28).

In reference to the accountability of taking a human life, God says, "Whoever sheds human blood, by humans shall their blood be shed; for in the image of God has God made mankind" (Genesis 9:6). Along with the same calling is also the affirmation that even after the fall, recognizing the comprehensive impact of sin in every person's life, people are still image bearers of the Creator God and therefore carry responsibility to act within the world in a manner that reflects the priorities and character of God.

SIN AND ITS CONSEQUENCES

Chapter Six
Reflection Questions

Key Point
Sin entered the world through one disobedient act and resulted in three universal consequences: sinful heart desires, fleshly lusts, and depraved minds.

---

1) What was the basic sin of Adam and Eve?
2) How does this consistent human desire to have our own way show up in everyday life?
3) Can you be good enough to offset your own rebellion?

Personal Perspective
Write your own reaction to the thoughts communicated within this chapter.

GRACE AND TRUTH

CHAPTER SEVEN

REDEMPTION AND RECONCILIATION

In response to humanity's sinful act and need to reconcile His creation to Himself, God chooses to reveal Himself to His creation in an amazing manner. Initially, God calls Abram to move away from his family and obediently follow God's plan and will. Genesis 12:1-3 contain this initial call,

"The Lord said to Abram, 'Leave your country, your people and your father's household and go to the land I will show you. I will make you into a great nation and I will bless you. I will make your name great, and you will be a blessing. I will bless those who bless you and curse those who curse you and all peoples on the earth will be blessed through you.'"

God changes Abram's name to Abraham, meaning "father of many" (Genesis 17), signifying the important role Abraham plays in beginning the redemptive acts of God for His creation.

Over the next many centuries, through

Abraham, Isaac, Jacob, and Joseph, Abraham's offspring grow and become a people too numerous to count. Scripture records that during Joseph's life, Abraham's offspring moved to Egypt in order to survive a famine in Canaan. Four hundred years later, the Israelites find themselves enslaved in Egypt. God raises Moses as a leader to emancipate these people from their enslavement in Egypt. The book of Exodus describes what takes place.

Through God's miraculous interventions, the people of Israel are freed from captivity and return to the land of Canaan where Abraham was initially led by God. During this journey—40 years in all—God provides to Moses and the people of Israel the Ten Commandments in order for the people to live in a manner consistent with the character and will of God. Because of the fall of humanity, God provided the law to teach the people of Israel how to act in accordance with His will and purpose. As described in Exodus 20:20, Moses communicates as he comes back from Mt. Sinai after receiving the Ten Commandments, "Do not be afraid. God has come to test you, so that the fear of God will be with you to keep you from sinning." The law provided the people of Israel an idea of what types of behavior honored and dishonored God. It provided an understanding of the character of God and what God desired initially for His creation. It also provided a complex sacrificial system where the sacrifice of animals paid the price for the sins committed by the people of Israel (Leviticus 1-10). The people of Israel all swore, "We will do everything the Lord has said" (Exodus 19:8).

You do not need to be even vaguely familiar with Old Testament Scripture to know it was not long until the people of Israel broke this oath. Throughout the history of Israel, Scripture shares numerous examples of women and men who walked faithfully with God, attempting to live according to God's law, as well as individuals who, as the author of the book of Judges writes, "each did as he saw fit" (Judges 21:25) with no regard of God or God's law. Even in the stories of the men and women who walked faithfully with God, Scripture is clear that not a single person ever lived in complete accordance with God's will and God's law. The ability for the nation of Israel to live by the requirements of the law was an abject failure. Within the course of the next several hundred years, the Kingdom of Israel is established, first with Saul as king, then David (1 & 2 Samuel). It soon splits into two kingdoms, Israel and Judah. As both nations fail to live by the requirements of the law, both nations are destroyed and the people taken into exile (1 & 2 Kings, 1 & 2 Chronicles). After 40 years of exile, a group of Israelites return to rebuild Jerusalem and once again attempt to carry out the requirements of the law (Ezra and Nehemiah).

Throughout this history, Old Testament Scripture is filled with prophecy concerning a coming Messiah who would save Israel and establish a kingdom that would never fail (Daniel, Isaiah, Micah, Psalms, Hosea, Zechariah, Jeremiah, Malachi, and more). When Jesus was born, the nation of Israel was a functioning nation, although occupied and controlled by the Roman Empire.

REDEMPTION AND RECONCILIATION

Two competing religious groups vied for the hearts and minds of the people. The Pharisees, who believed in the resurrection of the dead, worked diligently to uphold the entirety of God's law. The second group, the Sadducees, did not believe in the resurrection of the dead but also were interested in upholding God's law with broader and more liberal interpretation. Both groups desired the nation of Israel to be freed from its occupiers, as did several other groups of Israelites who worked diligently for the emancipation of Israel.

It is within this context that Jesus of Nazareth, the Messiah, is born to a virgin named Mary, who lived in Nazareth (Matthew 1-2, Luke 2). John 1:29 records the words spoken by John the Baptist regarding Jesus as John was calling for repentance and baptizing in the Jordan River. He proclaims, "Look, the Lamb of God, who takes away the sin of the world!" The difficulty the people of Israel had in recognizing Jesus of Nazareth as the Messiah or the Christ was because they were looking for a military leader who would bring victory over the occupying

Roman Empire and establish a prophesied earthly kingdom that would never end (Daniel).

Instead, Jesus the Christ came to establish an eternal kingdom that would never perish or fail. As Jesus stands trial before Pontius Pilate, Jesus states, "My kingdom is not of this world; if it were, My servants would fight to prevent My arrest by the Jews. But now My kingdom is not of this world" (John 18:36). As Jesus Christ, the true Messiah, offers Himself up freely to death, His sacrifice provides atonement for the sins of all humanity—past, present, and future. The author of Hebrews describes Jesus's atoning sacrifice,

"Every priest stands daily at his service, offering repeatedly the same sacrifices, which can never take away sins. But when Christ had offered for all time a single sacrifice for sins, He sat down at the right hand of God, waiting from that time until His enemies should be made a footstool for his feet. For by a single offering, He has perfected for all time those who are being sanctified" (Hebrews 10:11-14).

Through this act, God, who is holy, provides

REDEMPTION AND RECONCILIATION

the means for all of humanity to be restored into the relationship He intended when He initially created the heavens and the earth. Christ Jesus's sacrifice provides the means of redemption, where sins are forgiven, and reconciliation, where the relationship with God and His creation (all humanity) is restored to its initial condition.

First Peter 3:9 beautifully portrays God's desire in providing this means of restoring right relationship and forgiving the sins of His creation. Peter writes, "[God] is patient with you, not wanting anyone to perish, but everyone to come to repentance." An even more familiar verse communicating the same sentiment is John 3:16, "For this is how God loved the world: He gave His one and only Son, that whoever believes in Him should not perish but have eternal life." God's desire is that all of humanity be saved, and the means of making that potential a reality was through the willing sacrifice of His one and only Son, Jesus the Christ.

Chapter Seven
Reflection Questions

Key Point
God Himself provides for redemption and reconciliation through Christ Jesus's sacrifice.

---

1) Can you forgive someone without a cost? What did that forgiveness cost God?

2) How generous is God's plan? How should we respond?

3) How do you balance the reality of God's patience and forgiveness with God's desire for us to be obedient and holy? How do you live this out daily? How does it impact your interactions with family and those within your circle of influence?

Personal Perspective
Write your own reaction to the thoughts communicated within this chapter.

NOTES

GRACE AND TRUTH

CHAPTER EIGHT

THIS IS GRACE

Grace can only be understood once truth and its consequences are understood. God alone is holy. Romans 3:23 makes the truth plain in stating that all people "have sinned and fall short of the glory of God." Scripture continues to make this truth plain, communicating that the "wages of sin is death, but the gift of God is eternal life in Christ Jesus our Lord" (Romans 6:23). Grace simply means that instead of a person receiving what he/she deserves for the sinful life he/she has lived (death and condemnation), that person receives eternal life through Christ Jesus. Grace is receiving what you do not deserve.

While the desire of God – not wanting anyone to perish – is universal in its application, there is a single condition for an individual to receive grace: Belief. Again, John 3:16 states, "whoever believes in Him should not perish but have eternal life." The means of salvation is universal, but only those who believe are saved. Paul describes this commitment on the part of an individual in this manner, "If you declare with your mouth, 'Jesus is Lord,' and believe in your heart that God raised Him from the dead, you will be saved" (Romans 10:9). *Belief* is the only condition of salvation.

Belief, however, is stronger than mere acknowledgment. In James 2:19, the first-century leader of the early Christian church said, "You believe that there is one God. Good! Even the demons believe that – and shudder." Belief is neither acknowledgment nor intellectual understanding; it is accepting and subsequently orienting the entirety of one's life in response to that belief.

The story of Jesus raising Lazarus from the dead beautifully articulates this idea. Jesus intentionally delayed coming to Bethany when He heard that Lazarus was sick. Once Lazarus had died, Jesus arrives in Bethany and is met by Martha, Lazarus' sister. As Martha grieves to Jesus about Lazarus' death, He says to her, "I am the resurrection and the life. The one who believes in me will live, even though they die; and whoever lives by believing in me will never die. Do you believe this?" (John 11:25-26). Belief, in this context, requires the ascent of the mind (the acknowledgment of truth) leading to the volition of the will. The individual who "believes" submits his or her own individual will to the Lord and His will.

Consider Jesus's request of the Father on the night prior to His crucifixion. Luke 22:42 records the request, "Father, if you are willing, take this cup from me; yet not my will, but yours be done." Or Jesus's words to His disciples recorded in Luke 9:23, "Whoever wants to be my disciple must deny themselves and take up their cross daily and follow me." Belief is the single condition of salvation; however, it must be a comprehensive belief where the volition of a person's will is submitted to the will of God based upon the ascension of the mind in recognizing the validity of the claims that Jesus is the resurrection and the life.

This is grace. As a person believes, he/she is saved. Paul explains in Ephesians 2:8, "For it is by grace you have been saved, through faith – and this is not from yourselves, it is the gift of God – not by works, so that no one can boast." A person no longer must adhere to the significant ritual aspects of the Jewish law, nor must he or she attain absolute moral perfection, to gain salvation. Instead, salvation is a free gift to all who believe. If you believe, expressing faith in Jesus, you are saved. This is the good news of the Gospel message, as Paul writes in 2 Corinthians 5:19, "that God was reconciling the world to Himself in Christ, not counting people's sins against them." The only requirement of salvation is belief that Jesus is the Christ, the Son of the Living God.

Chapter Eight
Reflection Questions

Key Point
Belief requires assent of the mind, trust and submission of one's will and is by the grace of God.

---

1) Is there such a thing as "belief" without content – belief without a claim of truth?

2) Faith results in actions (works); faith is evidenced by works. Can you "work" without faith?

3) What is belief without subsequent action? Does lack of action reveal a lack of belief?

4) What is your role in your faith formation? What is God's role? How does that interplay impact your daily walk with God?

Personal Perspective
Write your own reaction to the thoughts communicated within this chapter.

GRACE AND TRUTH

CHAPTER NINE

RESPONSE TO MERCY: PERSONAL TRANSFORMATION

So then, the following question must be asked: How should a person, as a recipient of this amazing gift of grace, live? The apostle Paul's multiple letters to early Christian churches attempt to answer these questions, as do Peter's, John's, James's, and Jude's. In Romans 12, perhaps the clearest answer is recorded. Paul writes,

"Therefore, I urge you brothers, in view of God's mercy, to offer your bodies as a living sacrifice, holy and pleasing to God – this is your true and proper worship. Do not conform to the pattern of this world but be transformed by the renewing of your mind. Then you will be able to test and approve what God's will is – His good, pleasing and perfect will" (Romans 12:1-2).

Notice first—it is of primary importance—that Paul states this is in view of mercy, not to earn mercy. Mercy is the free gift from God to all who believe. In response, then, to this unbelievable gift, Paul says that Christians should offer themselves to God as living sacrifices. This may sound reminiscent of Jesus's statement to His disciples that they deny themselves, take up their crosses daily and follow Him (Matthew 16:24). This is exactly what Paul is imploring his readers to do: to live in a manner and way that serves and honors God, not yourself. In fact, Paul calls this type of life orientation worship. We often think worship is confined to times where Christians gather together to pray, sing, and praise God. Worship includes those activities, but those encompass only one aspect of worship. True, comprehensive worship is living the totality of one's life in a manner that submits to the will of God.

Paul continues then with an imperative command, "Do not conform to the pattern of this world" (Romans 12:2). What is the pattern of this world? Romans 1 contains a great description that has been described earlier. The consequences of not worshipping God but serving created things are (1) sinful desires of the heart, (2) shameful lusts, and

RESPONSE TO MERCY: PERSONAL TRANSFORMATION

(3) a depraved mind. (If you find it helpful, go back and reread the "Sin and Its Consequences" section unpacking the description of the pattern of the world.) Paul implores believers to no longer live in a manner reflective of the patterns of the world. Instead, Christians live differently as an appropriate response to mercy, not in order to earn mercy. Christians are to live differently than the world lives.

Returning to Carl Trueman's description of expressive individualism, our broader world believes acting in manners and ways most consistent to a person's innate desires and proclivities. As Paul makes clear in this passage, Christians should not orient their lives around what is most innately part of themselves or their deepest fallen proclivities or inclinations. Instead, Christians are to offer themselves as "living sacrifices" and no longer live in the typical fashion of the world. This requires a complete transformation encompassing a change of life, of purpose, and of identity.

In 1 Corinthians 6:19-20, Paul writes, "Do you not know that your bodies are temples of the

Holy Spirit, who is in you, whom you have received from God? You are not your own; you were bought at a price. Therefore, honor God with your bodies." A proper response to mercy is living in a manner that reflects the character and the will of God. This transformation, or process of sanctification, can take a long time, but Christians, throughout their lifetime, should see a progression of living less and less like the world does and more and more in ways reflecting God's desires and character.

As a Christian attempts to avoid living according to the patterns of the world in favor of transformation by the renewing of the mind, the Christian's ability to test and approve God's "good, perfect, and pleasing will" increases (Romans 8). This process of transforming the mind to know God's will is called sanctification. Paul describes it in this way, "For those God foreknew He also predestined to be conformed to the image of His Son, that He might be the firstborn among many brothers and sisters" (Romans 8:29). All people are born into sin and live in ways that are consistent with the

RESPONSE TO MERCY: PERSONAL TRANSFORMATION

patterns of the world. After a person receives mercy, through our faith (belief) in Christ, the process of our transformation begins.

As we attempt to live according to God's will rather than according to the patterns of the world, we are changed and conformed more and more into the image of Jesus Christ Himself. This does not mean that we become God, but that our lives reflect His character and purpose instead of our own. We no longer live for ourselves and our own individual desires or will, but instead we live in a manner that is in line with the life of Jesus Christ. Eventually, as Romans 8:29 articulates, this transformation will be complete and total. Christians, through this process of transformation or sanctification, will be conformed to the image of Christ Jesus and clearly understand and live according to God's good, pleasing, and perfect will.

Chapter Nine
Reflection Questions

Key Point
Through and in view of God's mercy, lives change.

---

1) In what ways are elements of expressive individualism observed within culture?

2) Now that we are reconciled to God, back in His family, how should our lives change?

3) Are there appropriate ways to respond when we see other believers living in ways that do not "serve and honor God"?

4) How do we encourage and inspire the next generation to be courageous in their rejection of the self-serving world and embracing God-honoring lives of Christian character?

Personal Perspective
Write your own reaction to the thoughts communicated within this chapter.

NOTES

GRACE AND TRUTH

CHAPTER TEN

THE HOLY SPIRIT AND SANCTIFICATION

This may seem to be a daunting—perhaps even impossible—task. Consider the lesson Jesus taught his disciples concerning the difficulty of the rich entering the kingdom of God. Matthew 19:24 records His statement, "Again I tell you, it is easier for a camel to go through the eye of a needle than for someone who is rich to enter the kingdom of God." Jesus goes on to communicate, however, "With man this is impossible, but with God all things are possible" (Matthew 19:26). Christians are not left on their own to pursue their own transformation, but the Holy Spirit is with us, indwelling us, teaching us, convicting us and aiding in the process of our sanctification (John 14; John 16; 1 Corinthians 2; Romans 8; Titus 3). As Jesus was providing His last words to His disciples, He asks them to stay in Jerusalem "until you have been clothed with power from on high" (Luke 24:49). Luke goes on to communicate the coming of the Holy Spirit as he describes the day of Pentecost in Acts 2:1-4,

> *"When the day of Pentecost came, they were all together in one place. Suddenly a sound like the blowing of a violent wind came from heaven and filed the whole house where they were sitting. They saw what seemed to be tongues of fire that separated and came to rest on each of them. All of them were filed with the Holy Spirit and began to speak in other tongues (languages) as the Spirit enabled them."*

Those who were in Jerusalem to celebrate the Passover reacted in utter amazement. They asked, "Aren't all these who are speaking Galileans? Then how is it that each of us hears them in our native language?" (Acts 2:7-8). Luke then records 16 different countries or regions from where people had come for the Passover Festival who then heard the Gospel message proclaimed in their own native language. Peter addresses the crowd, and Luke records that more than 3,000 people were baptized that day (Luke 2:41). The Holy Spirit provides the power and ability for Christians not only to share their faith but also to grow in faith.

THE HOLY SPIRIT AND SANCTIFICATION

Jesus communicated to His disciples that the Holy Spirit will "teach you all things and remind you of everything I have said to you" (John 14:26). Galatians 5 describes how the Holy Spirit teaches and reminds us, aiding in our transformation from living lives consistent with the patterns of the world into men and women who live in ways consistent with the character of God and His intent for His creation. Paul writes,

"So I say, walk by the Spirit, and you will not gratify the desires of the flesh. For the flesh craves what is contrary to the Spirit, and the Spirit what is contrary to the flesh. They are opposed to each other, so that you do not do what you want. But if you are led by the Spirit, you are not under the law.

"The acts of the flesh are obvious: sexual immorality, impurity, debauchery; idolatry and sorcery; hatred, discord, jealousy, and rage; rivalries, divisions, factions and envy; drunkenness, orgies and the like. I warn you, as I did before, that those who practice such things will not inherit the kingdom of God.

"But the fruit of the Spirit is love, joy,

peace, patience, kindness, goodness, faithfulness, gentleness, and self-control. Against such things there is no law. Those who belong to Christ Jesus have crucified the flesh with its passions and desires. Since we live by the Spirit, let us walk in step with the Spirit. Let us not become conceited, provoking and envying one another" (Galatians 5:16-25).

One of the first things Paul desires to communicate to the Christians living in Galatia: If Christians are led by the Spirit, they are not under the law. Returning to the requirement of salvation, people receive salvation as a free gift from God through faith in Christ Jesus. Christians are not under the law. However, this does not provide license to live and act in any way a person wants. God desires His children to live in ways that reflect His character and will, so Paul explains in this passage the difference between a life that is consistent and a life that is inconsistent with the character and will of God. Through the process of sanctification, the Holy Spirit aids believers in walking in obedience to God's will, in ways that are consistent with God's character and in ways that aid in accomplishing the will and plans of God.

While a Christian's life within this world experiences significant transformation, our complete transformation will occur at the second coming of Christ. In Romans 7, Paul describes the internal struggle Christians experience as they attempt to put off their "old self," which lived in manners consistent with the patterns of the world, and live instead by the Spirit. He writes,

> *"I do not understand what I do. For what I want to do I do not do, but what I hate, I do. And if I do what I do not want to do, I agree that the law is good. As it is, it is no long I, myself, who do it, but it is sin living in me. For I know that good itself does not dwell in me, that is, in my sinful nature. For I have the desire to do what is good, but I cannot carry it out. For I do not do the good I want to do, but the evil I do not want to do – this I keep on doing. Now if I do what I do not want to do, it is no longer I who do it, but sin living in me that does it"* (Romans 7:15-20).

The reality is, as long as we are living in this world, temptations and the lure of the world can impact us. Even deeply committed Christian men and women sin. Paul, in a beautiful moment of vulnerability, confesses that he still, at times, chooses to act in ways that are consistent with the patterns of the world rather than the character and will of God. However, the longer a person walks closely with God, his or her life should reflect with increasing clarity and consistency the character and will of God. When Christ comes again, our transformation becomes complete. Paul, at the conclusion of 1 Corinthians 15, communicates this beautifully. He writes,

> *"I declare to you, brothers and sisters, that flesh and blood cannot inherit the kingdom of God, nor does the perishable inherit the imperishable. Listen, I tell you a mystery: We will not all sleep, but we will all be changed – in a flash, in the twinkling of an eye, at the last trumpet. For the trumpet will sound, the dead will be raised imperishable, and the mortal with immortality. When the perishable has been clothed with the*

imperishable, and the mortal with immortality, then the saying that is written will come true:

"'Where, O death, is your victory? Where, O death, is your sting?'

"The sting of death is sin, and the power of sin is the law. But thanks be to God! He gives us the victory through our Lord Jesus Christ" (1 Corinthians 15:50-57).

When Christ comes again, death will be swallowed up in victory. At this point, we will be changed in order to spend eternity with the God of all creation. This is the promise of our faith in Christ and the hope of all Christians.

Chapter Ten
Reflection Questions

Key Point
Through the power of the Holy Spirit working in and through the life of a Christian, a Christian can live in a manner that reflects the priorities of Jesus.

1) What do you know of the purpose and role of the Holy Spirit in the life of a Christian?
2) Can a person live in ways expressing the Fruit of the Spirit without the Holy Spirit?
3) What are the greatest challenges or obstacles within our current world impeding your ability to live in a manner consistent with the Fruit of the Spirit?

Personal Perspective
Write your own reaction to the thoughts communicated within this chapter.

NOTES

GRACE AND TRUTH

CHAPTER ELEVEN

AMBASSADORS OF CHRIST

While we await the glorious day that Christ returns, Paul reminds Christians of our purpose as he concludes his thoughts in 1 Corinthians 15:58. He writes, "Therefore, my brothers and sisters, stand firm. Let nothing move you. Always give yourselves fully to the work of the Lord, because you know that your labor in the Lord is not in vain." Consider Paul's admonition to "give yourselves fully to the work of the Lord." Implicit within that statement exists the idea that we are somehow asked to participate in the work of God in our world.

The very last recorded words of Jesus to His disciples as He was ascending into heaven after His resurrection are recorded in Matthew 28:18-20. Matthew writes, "All authority in heaven and on earth has been given to me. Therefore, go and make disciples of all nations, baptizing them in the name of the Father and of the Son and of the Holy Spirit, and teaching them to obey everything I have commanded you. And surely, I am with you always, to the very end of the age." This passage is known as the Great Commission, the call of Jesus's disciples to take the message of the Gospel to the world. This commissioning of Jesus's disciples extends to all followers of Christ.

Paul also describes participation in the work of God in 2 Corinthians 5,

"For Christ's love compels us, because we are convinced that one died for all, and therefore all died. And He died for all, that those who live should no longer live for themselves but for Him who died for them and was raised again. So, from now on we regard no one from a worldly point of view. Though we once regarded Christ in this way, we do so no longer. Therefore, if anyone is in Christ, the new creation has come: the old has gone, the new has come. All this is from God who reconciled us to Himself through Christ and gave us the ministry of reconciliation: that God was reconciling the world to Himself in Christ, not counting people's sins against them. And He has committed to us the message of reconciliation. We are therefore Christ's ambassadors, as though

God were making His appeal through us" (2 Corinthians 5:14- 20).

Within this passage Paul reminds the church in Corinth of the Gospel message as well as the appropriate response of a Christian to mercy, "that those who live should no longer live for themselves but for Him who died for them and was raised again." Then he communicates what Jesus commanded in the Great Commission, that we, as recipients of salvation, are asked to serve as ambassadors of Christ to the world. All Christians, regardless of their profession, stage of life, or perceived giftedness, are representatives of Christ to the world.

Henri Nouwen, a former university professor and Roman Catholic Priest, stated in his book *In the Name of Jesus* one of my all-time favorite statements,

"We are not the healers, we are not the reconcilers, we are not the givers of life. We are sinful, broken, vulnerable people who need as much care as anyone we care for. The mystery of ministry is that we have been chosen to make our own limited and very conditional love the gateway for the unlimited and unconditional

love of God" (pg. 62).

While we are not perfect, we are God's chosen instrument to proclaim to the world the message of the Gospel, that God is not counting humanity's sins against them. This is the message of redemption and reconciliation.

Chapter Eleven
Reflection Questions

Key Point
We are God's instrument to proclaim the Gospel.

---

1) How should we tell others about this great gift and praise the giver?
2) Through the gospel, we have reconciliation and eternal life. Which is of greater importance?
3) Should our fulfillment of God's work in the world change based on our desire in the moment – or during a longer-lasting low point in our faith journey?

Personal Perspective
Write your own reaction to the thoughts communicated within this chapter.

GRACE AND TRUTH

CHAPTER TWELVE

GOSPEL = GRACE + TRUTH

So how do we, as recipients of mercy and therefore redeemed and reconciled individuals, take the Gospel message to our world? Christians reflect the character and the will of God; therefore, we should bring the Gospel to the world, just as Jesus did, "full of grace and truth" (John 1:14). Today our world is polarized. Regardless of the issue, a moderate path is rarely found. Jesus found Himself in a similar scenario two millennia ago. On the one hand, the Pharisees worked diligently to ensure the people of Israel followed the law closely. It was their highest priority; they even challenged Jesus several times for not abiding by the law. Mark 2:23-28 records one such encounter. Jesus and His disciples were walking along grainfields. As they walked, they began to pick some heads of grain and eat them. The Pharisees questioned Jesus and asked, "Look, why are they doing what is unlawful on the Sabbath?" (Mark 2:24). Jesus's response is that "the Sabbath was made for man, not man for the Sabbath. So the Son of Man is Lord even of the Sabbath" (Mark 2:27-28).

On the other hand, many in Israel at that time lived in ways reflecting the priorities of the Roman Empire rather than Jewish tradition and law. Perhaps the best example of an individual within this category was Herod Antipas, who was the king of Israel during the life of Jesus. Herod is the family name of several rulers of Israel during the Roman Empire's reign. Herod had little to no regard for the law. He was a pragmatist who did what was best for him and his own success. Herod Antipas divorced his wife and married Herodias, the wife of his brother. The book of Luke describes this event and the fact that John the Baptist preached against these actions, which led Herod Antipas to throw John the Baptist in prison (Luke 3) and, as Matthew records, to eventually execute him (Matthew 14). As Jesus stood trial prior to His crucifixion, Herod could finally meet Jesus face-to-face. Luke records, "When Herod saw Jesus, he was greatly pleased, because for a long time he had been wanting to see him. From what he had heard about him, he hoped to see him perform a sign of some sort" (Luke 23:8). Herod Antipas had little interest in things beyond his immediate gratification and pleasure. Jesus would be fun to meet, as long as He was entertaining.

Our current world reflects these same polarized perspectives. On the one hand, there are many who defend the truth of God with vigor and righteous indignation. On the other hand, there are those who have little regard for God beyond what God can do to bless their lives. After Jesus feeds 4,000, recorded in Mark 8, He and His disciples are in a boat crossing the Sea of Galilee. Jesus says to them, "Be careful. Watch out for the yeast of the Pharisees and that of Herod" (Mark 8:15). The Gospel message is not a message of the politically right or the politically left. The Gospel message is a path that brings all people together with an invitation to pursue God.

Returning to John 1:14, Jesus came into the world "full of grace and truth." Without the combination of both grace and truth, the message of the Gospel is perverted. The elevation of truth over grace, or the elevation of grace over truth, leads to division and a misunderstanding of who God is and what He has done in creating and redeeming His world. The Gospel is only represented fully and as Christ Jesus desires if it is proclaimed with both grace and truth.

Consider for a moment truth without grace. It was the world of the Pharisees and is often seen in today's Christian circles. I was raised in the Free Methodist Church and am extremely thankful for the heritage of this wonderful denomination. The genesis of the Free Methodist Church is a powerful story. It is a story of emancipation; it is a story of men and women coming together and decrying the terrible practice of slavery in the United States. In fact, the men and women that led this charge of emancipation were kicked out of their church (the Methodist Episcopal Church) because of their stance on the abolition of slavery. Therefore, the obvious name of this new denomination was the Free

Methodist Church. But within this tremendously important rationale for founding the denomination, an interesting thing also occurred: A deep element of legalism came along with their desire for all people to be free.

So, as a young man being raised in the Free Methodist Church, my parents were seen as extremely progressive because they allowed me to go to high school dances and to watch movies. In fact, I remember a scenario that played out at my identical twin brother's wedding reception expressing this reality beautifully well. He decided to marry a young lady who was raised in the Lutheran church. As the plans for their day began to take shape, they decided to have an open bar and a dance at the reception. In wonderful deference to our new extended family, we quietly agreed to acquiesce.

It was a marvelous ceremony, and as the reception began, all were having a grand time. I remember seeing my very pious and lovely Grandma Dufloth as we danced. She was such an elegant woman who took her faith extremely seriously. I also remember, as a young boy, seeing her fervently praying on her knees for our family and others. She often spoke about what she was learning in her study of the Bible as she read daily from Scripture. She also lived and modeled grace extremely well, so this is not a condemnation of my Grandma Dufloth.

As my brother's reception took place, my siblings and our friends joyously danced as my Grandma Dufloth sat right on the edge of the dance floor, watching with a huge smile on her face. I thought, "What a wonderful, beautiful woman." I decided to go ask my grandma if she would like to dance with me. I knew she had never danced in a setting like this, so perhaps my invitation would provide her the impetus to join her family in celebration. Boldly, I approached her and asked, "Grandma, would you dance with me?" She looked up at me, so dignified and beautiful. With a smile and full of grace, she said, "Oh, honey, I would feel like such a hypocrite." How sad. She lost a tremendous opportunity to participate in something that she dearly wanted to be a part of, but her perspective of truth limited her ability to enjoy something that was absolutely pleasing to God.

When truth is not coupled with grace, it is harsh, it is demanding, it is burdensome, and it leads to legalism and condemnation. John 3:17 states, "For God did not send His Son into the world to condemn the world, but to save it through Him." Jesus also teaches, "Take my yoke upon you and learn from me, for I am gentle and humble in heart, and you will find rest for your souls" (Matthew 11:29). Contrast that picture with His statements to the Pharisees, "They tie up heavy, cumbersome loads and put them on other people's shoulders, but they themselves are not willing to lift a finger to move them" (Matthew 23:4). Many within our modern culture believe this is exactly what Christianity represents. Christians are understood to be judgmental and even bigoted. Our defense of the sanctity of life or of a biblical view of marriage can come across as harsh unless it is also presented with an equal amount of grace. Truth without grace is heavy and burdensome, robs hope and joy from yourself and others, and is not a full representation of the Gospel message.

Grace without truth, on the other hand, leads to the relativism common within our world today. With no grounding in truth, people merely stay within their depravity and sinfulness, never truly understanding from what they are being saved. The deception here is great: Many believe they are pursuing the best for their lives, yet they are merely chasing after things that are patterned after this world and will therefore perish. Grace is a wonderful concept, but without truth it has no context to provide meaning, substance, or the transformation of individuals. Consider Jude's letter in the New Testament. He writes, "Certain men whose condemnation was written about long ago have secretly slipped in among you. They are godless men who pervert the grace of our God into a license for immorality" (Jude 1:4).

What we are experiencing within our world, within these pendulum swings of legalism to unbridled freedom and moral relativism, is not new but something as ancient as the Gospel message itself. Grace must be accompanied by truth or it is not the Gospel. Paul's letter to the Galatians, as discussed earlier, clearly shows and demonstrates the idea of how truth comes together with grace to transform lives. Paul writes, "So I say, walk by the Spirit and you will not gratify the desires of the flesh" (Galatians 5:16). The word "flesh" is referring to the sin nature that is present within every person who has ever walked the face of the earth. Those things that are innate, those things that are most foundational and fundamental to each person, are described in the Bible as "flesh." We all are born with various proclivities and inclinations. While our culture today promotes these carnal desires as one's authentic self (I was born this way), the Bible instead clearly teaches that these propensities are indicative of a person's "flesh" or sin nature. Consider Paul's statement in his letter to the church in Ephesus,

> *"As for you, you were dead in your transgressions and sins, in which you used to live when you conformed to the ways of this world and of the ruler of the power of the air, the spirit who is now at work in the sons of disobedience. All of*

us also lived among them at one time, gratifying the cravings of our flesh and indulging its desires and thoughts. Like the rest, we were by nature children of wrath" (Ephesians 2:1-3).

Christianity teaches that, left to ourselves, we are by our own personal nature "objects of wrath." This means the desires, thoughts, and motives derived from the natural self are often contrary to the purpose and will of God. Again, as Paul states, "We are by nature children of wrath" (Ephesians 2:2). This is precisely the reason every person is desperately in need of God's grace and mercy. If left to our own nature, that which comes naturally to every person, we could never live in a manner that reflects God's will and purpose. Instead, we would only move deeper and deeper into our sinfulness and depravity, that which we all are by our own nature.

Paul continues in Galatians 5, describing the personal transformation available to those who accept the free gift of God's grace,

"So if you walk by the Spirit, you will not gratify the desires of the flesh, for the flesh desires

what is contrary to the Spirit and the Spirit what is contrary to the flesh. They are in conflict with each other, so you are not to do whatever you want" (Galatians 5:16-17).

This is the core of Christian discipline: Committing to live in a manner and way that reflects the character and the intent of the Creator God rather than living in a manner and a way that reflects the character and the patterns of our world. Paul continues,

"But if you are led by the Spirit, you are not under law, so the acts of the flesh are obvious. Sexual immorality, impurity, debauchery, idolatry, witchcraft, hatred, discord, jealousy, fits of rage, selfish ambition, dissensions, factions, envy, drunkenness, orgies, and the like. I warn you, as I did before, that those who live like this will not inherit the Kingdom of God" (Galatians 5:18-21).

The Gospel message of grace that is grounded in and married to truth calls people to live in manners that are different than the broader patterns and character of our world. There must be change. Paul continues, "But the fruit of the Spirit, however, is this, love, joy, peace, long suffering, kindness, goodness, faithfulness, gentleness, and self-control and against such things there is no law" (Galatians 5:22-23). Grace must be accompanied by truth to represent the full scope of the Gospel message of Jesus Christ and to provide the individual transformation offered to those who accept Christ Jesus as Lord.

The Gospel message brings both ideas together: Grace *and* Truth. One without the other is not gospel; it is a perversion of the gospel. The gospel message brings both grace and truth together and is expressed beautifully in the life and ministry of Jesus. Jesus's disciple, John, records an encounter with a woman who was caught in adultery, written in Chapter 8 of his gospel. John records that as Jesus walks into this situation, He sees the teachers of the law and the Pharisees with this particular woman that they have caught in the act of adultery. Jewish law required that she would be stoned and put to death. Leviticus 20:10 states, "If a man commits adultery with another man's wife – with the wife of his neighbor – both the adulterer and the adulteress are to be put to death."

So, the teachers of the law and the Pharisees decide to test Jesus's commitment to truth. Will He be faithful to the law? Will He be faithful to truth? So, they bring the woman to Jesus and they say, "Teacher, this woman was caught in the act of adultery. In the Law Moses commanded us to stone such a woman. Now, what shall be done with her?" (John 8:4-5).

Jesus responds in a way that amazed those who defend only truth. He bends down and begins to draw something in the sand. Commentators through the ages have conjectured concerning what Jesus drew. Some guess Jesus wrote out the Ten Commandments. Other commentators believe He listed particular sins committed by the teachers of the law, the Pharisees and those gathered in the crowd, waiting to see the outcome of this confrontation. The reality is, we do not know what Jesus drew in the sand, but ultimately He looks up and says, "Let any of you who is without sin, cast the first stone"

(John 8:7). Jesus then bends back down and begins to draw in the sand once again. As Jesus draws in the sand, the people who were gathered drop their stones and walk away, one by one. Eventually, only Jesus and the adulterous woman remain.

Jesus then turns His attention to her and asks a question, "Woman, where are they? Has no one condemned you?" She responds, "There is no one here who condemns me." Jesus responds in grace saying, "Then neither do I condemn you." But He does not stop only with grace. He then moves to truth, "So go and sin no more" (John 8:10-11). Jesus loved this woman. He did not want her to remain in her depravity and sinful state. Grace offered forgiveness, and truth offered complete restoration to God's will. One without the other is not the Gospel.

The Gospel message is a message of both grace and truth. Grace without truth leads to relativism and the promotion of immorality in ways that are inconsistent with the patterns of the Holy Spirit and the intent of God's will enacted in His creation. But truth without grace is a distortion of the Gospel with catastrophic consequences of legalism, heavy burdens, and difficulty. The description of the Gospel contained in 2 Corinthians 5 communicates that God is not counting humanity's sins against them. It is a message of extreme grace, coupled with absolute truth. At Spring Arbor University we strive to educate our students and live ourselves as "critical participants in the contemporary world"—according to SAU's Concept. In doing so, our model and presentation of the Gospel must be the full and complete Gospel. It must be the Gospel brought through Christ Jesus as He came into the world full of grace and truth. This Gospel message does not elevate one over the other but brings both grace and truth together as an integrated message of redemption and reconciliation and a call for us to pursue God's will, God's character, and God's intent for His creation over the character and the patterns of our world in which we live.

Chapter Twelve
Reflection Questions

Key Point
The Gospel is both grace *and* truth.

---

1) What would truth without grace be? What examples of truth without grace have you observed?
2) What would grace without truth be? What examples of grace without truth have you observed?
3) Have you personally experienced a scenario where both truth and grace were communicated or demonstrated well?

Personal Perspective
Write your own reaction to the thoughts communicated within this chapter.

NOTES

GRACE AND TRUTH

REFERENCES

Anselm of Canterbury. (2008). *Why God Became Man, in Anselm of Canterbury: The Major Works.* Oxford University Press.

Free Methodist Book of Discipline. (2015). https://fmcusa.org/wp-content/uploads/2015-Book-Of-Discipline-Pages1.pdf

Holy Bible. (2011). New International Version. Zondervan.

Josephus, Flavius. (93). *Antiquities of the Jews.* https://www.gutenberg.org/files/2848/2848-h/2848-h.htm

Lausanne Covenant. (1975). https://lausanne.org/content/covenant/lausanne-covenant#cov

Lewis, C.S. (1952). *Mere Christianity.* Macmillan Publishing Company, Incorporated.

Nouwen, Henri. (1989). *In the Name of Jesus.* The Crossroad Publishing Company

Tacitus. (109). Annals.

Tennent, Timothy. (2020). *For the Body: Recovering a Theology of Gender, Sexuality, and the Human Body.* Zondervan.

Trueman, Carl R. (2020). *The Rise and Triumph of the Modern Self: Cultural Amnesia, Expressive Individualism, and the Road to Sexual Revolution.* Crossway.